retribution forthcoming

Hollis Summers Poetry Prize

GENERAL EDITOR: SARAH GREEN

Named after the distinguished poet who taught for many years at Ohio University and made Athens, Ohio, the subject of many of his poems, this competition invites writers to submit unpublished collections of original poems. The competition is open to poets who have not published a book-length collection as well as to those who have.

Full and updated information is available on the Hollis Summers Poetry Prize web page: ohioswallow.com/poetry_prize.

Meredith Carson, *Infinite Morning*
Memye Curtis Tucker, *The Watchers*
V. Penelope Pelizzon, *Nostos*
Kwame Dawes, *Midland*
Allison Eir Jenks, *The Palace of Bones*
Robert B. Shaw, *Solving for X*
Dan Lechay, *The Quarry*
Joshua Mehigan, *The Optimist*
Jennifer Rose, *Hometown for an Hour*
Ann Hudson, *The Armillary Sphere*
Roger Sedarat, *Dear Regime: Letters to the Islamic Republic*
Jason Gray, *Photographing Eden*
Will Wells, *Unsettled Accounts*
Stephen Kampa, *Cracks in the Invisible*
Nick Norwood, *Gravel and Hawk*
Charles Hood, *South × South: Poems from Antarctica*
Alison Powell, *On the Desire to Levitate*
Shane Seely, *The Surface of the Lit World*
Michelle Y. Burke, *Animal Purpose*
Michael Shewmaker, *Penumbra*
Idris Anderson, *Doubtful Harbor*
Joseph J. Capista, *Intrusive Beauty*
Julie Hanson, *The Audible and the Evident*
Fleda Brown, *Flying through a Hole in the Storm*
Sara Henning, *Terra Incognita*
Andrew Collard, *Sprawl*
Katie Berta, *retribution forthcoming*

retribution forthcoming

poems

Katie Berta

OHIO UNIVERSITY PRESS

ATHENS

Ohio University Press, Athens, Ohio 45701
ohioswallow.com
© 2024 by Ohio University Press

To obtain permission to quote, reprint, or otherwise reproduce or distribute material
from Ohio University Press publications, please contact our rights and permissions
department at (740) 593-1154 or (740) 593-4536 (fax).

Printed in the United States of America
Ohio University Press books are printed on acid-free paper ∞ ™

Library of Congress Cataloging-in-Publication Data
Names: Berta, Katie, 1986– author.
Title: Retribution forthcoming : poems / Katie Berta.
Description: Athens : Ohio University Press, 2024. | Series: Hollis Summers poetry prize
Identifiers: LCCN 2023043239 (print) | LCCN 2023043240 (ebook) | ISBN 9780821411506
    (paperback ; acid-free paper) | ISBN 9780821447604 (pdf)
Subjects: BISAC: POETRY / Women Authors | LCGFT: Poetry.
Classification: LCC PS3602.E768254 R48 2024 (print) | LCC PS3602.E768254 (ebook) |
    DDC 811/.6—dc23/eng/20231121
LC record available at https://lccn.loc.gov/2023043239
LC ebook record available at https://lccn.loc.gov/2023043240

To Kent,
whose name and likeness appear
all over this book

To combat the resistances of language you must keep
   talking my analyst tells me.

—*Anne Carson*

Can you tell me I'm worse than others?
OK, yes, I'm worse than others, but can you say I'm the worst
   of all?

—*Chelsey Minnis*

Contents

//

///

Compact

No agreement undergirds the world.
If you don't believe me, just try asking for something.

I know, I shouldn't be bitter. Being's a balance:
trying to convince myself I'm valuable

while believing I deserve nothing.
As a child I had nothing.

Someone—you, god?—put me in a room alone
and left me there. When our dog locks himself

in my boyfriend's office while we're gone,
he chews the clothes Kent leaves on the floor

to smithereens, maybe to keep himself from chewing
himself. Asking questions of god is, of course, chewing

yourself. Though, in some situations it's practical.
Like when some part of you is
what's caught.

The rattlesnakes they keep in the life sciences
building remind me of my dog—

the way they lay their chins on a rock to get a minute of rest, the way
their eyes get heavily lidded as they stare off out of their tanks—
but so do the dead mice (one rat) littering their cages around noon, their little bodies
curled around some unseen center, their tiny, ratty feet with scales just like
the rattlesnakes'. There they are: mammals. Same team as me. The biggest snake
is an albino so huge his scales, when they lift from his body
as he curls around a rock or rodent, look like big, dry flakes of oatmeal.
I have trouble relating to snakes. This one, if we met him in our yard, would pump
so much poison into my dog's leg, he'd lie down yelping, curling like
one of the pre-killed mice onto his tummy, protecting what's left. I can't think of my dog
dying in front of me in the yard without wanting to chop this snake to pieces
with a shovel, but when I see him here, bored, he makes me think of a dog sleeping,
not dying. I had to stop watching nature shows because of this—not knowing who
to relate to—used to root for the prey not the predator but
the wolf pups die, too, if they don't get anything to eat, the lion cubs, the killer
whales. Thinking this way inevitably makes you cry helplessly in the dark,
the blue light of the television's vast sea, full of creatures vying for *this*,
this thing you're doing even as you just sit here, washing over you,
drowning you. Yes, inevitable is right. I know someone has to die.
All of us, in fact. I just wish the dog could live. The rats, too, the snake, me.

Everything we eat used to be alive, or still is,

the guy on NPR says. He says carrots are still living
when you bite into them, that they still have the wherewithal
to release a chemical signal warning the other carrots
of your descending mouth so they may try
to burrow their roots into the root-proof, soilless crisper
of your fridge. You can't help but feel a little cannibalistic
when you hear it, even as you virtuously chomp
into your super-dead steak, the other thing you're eating
for dinner.
                    (This isn't a poem about being a vegan, by the by,
but rather a poem about consciousnesses, the different types of them, or
what counts as one.)
                              Your beautiful steak, with the velvet-soft
fur on the end of its nose and its wet wet eyes watching
watching. A cow is a type of consciousness, too,
that we know nothing about. Inside her: a wordless, slow
place made of smells. Or—her interior—a wordless blood place
made of meat. But each of *us* is, basically, that same kind
of thing, no matter what nomenclature. Human *beings*,
we stress, desperate to differentiate ourselves. The cow
is being, too, until she's not. Standing in a field at sunrise,
she takes a shit without even realizing it. She thinks,
The grass is wet the sun is brown like a spot on my baby
I am hungry woman soft I am grass field mother clover.

The clover thinks a zap of chemicals over to some other
clover—*Watch out for that fucking cow.*
                                        The blades of grass,
too numerous to even consider—the grass the grass the grass

Meat

You, too,
would curl, darken,
solidify
under pressure of heat

the two tendrils
of octopus on your plate
might remind you.

Delicacy
depends on the measure
of pain
it allows us
to ignore—the complicated
embroidery for which some
young woman's fingers
had to callous.
The pleasure we get from
the dress, when she finishes:
the fruit
of the meat
of a brain
so like the ones scrambled
with eggs or cut out
with the animal's tongue
and eaten
or covered
in cheese or capers
or chili sauce.

It's like
the way you decide a steak is done:
by comparing its tenderness
to the palm of your hand,
the part just under your thumb.
Or the way
your body becomes fragments,
butchered,
when some man yells
to you
from across a street.

How does it feel to be a harvest?
How does it feel to be
meat? You are a luxury,
but it does not feel
luxurious.

What does the octopus feel
before he's caught?
Before, the octopus was consumed
with cracking open the crab
he'd captured on the bed
of his reef.
All the octopus's thoughts
were consumed
by meat.

A magazine article is trying to convince me the bags under my eyes equal cell death,

which means I haven't been eating my vegetables, which is a moral failing.
The bags under my eyes, the mortality of each little cell.
In the magazine, it teaches you to apply concealer over the bags,
apply long wings onto your eyelids, which I do, though I know they are anti-academic.
I know enough about academia to know I'd like to wear my opposition to it
on my face. Diane Seuss says eyeliner is war. She affirms the middle of the country.
At a conference, the other writers keep saying the word "hillbilly," which I honestly think of
as a slur. Debating whether the poor are stupid or just gullible. Debating whether
they can be saved. My mother's family packed into their tiny house. Something about it
felt like a secret when I was a kid. Now, I eat my vegetables. Or I try. The pictures of women
with tiny bodies and perfect skin. Or are they girls? Someone at the conference
says the young look clean. The graduate students. Their skin a sort of luminous
halo surrounding their bodies. The young and the rich, anyway. In my PhD,
Sarah said we all aged like Barack Obama. All that stress. Think about that,
but for your whole life. Think about that but without all the—whatever it was we
had. Going to someone's house and eating the kale they cooked. The way
we believed it was all in service of such seriousness. Little did we know.
It was like you are to me, at arm's length. Believing you are serious. More serious
than others. Others toil to buy the larger-screen television. You toil to—
what? It's a more nebulous appreciation you're seeking. But it's all the same
impulse. Even the rich eat Taco Bell when they're drunk. One
of the best lessons of my education. Even the rich get fat if you stress
them out enough. Luminous skin aging like a president's. The cleanness
of the skin becoming otherwise. Fighting against my pores. Fighting
to thin my body. Believing beauty, richness, smartness is a kind of morality.
A kind of mortality. Just because you live doesn't mean you're good. Just being—
just being beautiful. The right kind of beauty. Worn on the outside,
they tell us, to show us what we might find within.

I realized skin care would not save my life,

that it wouldn't even save my face, and slowly my fervor
for it died. Stopped watching the videos in which women
would cup their hands into a white basin of water to simulate
their evening routine, to wash their faces of the colored wax
they'd applied to them just for their videos, of their detergents and oils.
Stopped patting the water from the shower into my cheeks,
tapping never pulling, patiently pressing. The cheek
a sunken cheek, the skin a gray corpsish skin. A cheek
no hydrator can revive. And in the mirror I see a gray corpsish
face, the kind of face that, if found at the foot of a stair
or curled stiffly around the lily mouth of a toilet bowl,
would signal its owner has ceased to be. Being
old is fine, if no one can tell. But they obviously can. Being
ugly has no particular meaning attached to it
until some other person enters the room. Hard not to
crumble under the gaze, knowing what they see. Or
thinking I know. No, it is intractable—the direction
I'm moving in, intractably. A crepiness turns
into something you can stick your finger through,
to your horror, and they're marketing you argan oil.
Lasers. Telling you to roll out the skin under your eyes
with jade. Staring at yourself in the mirror
as you wipe it all on feels more like dying than dying.
Feels as ugly as you feel, feeling your doom as you are.
Looking out from its gelid eye.

Cosmopolitan

When I was eleven or twelve years old
in one of the issues I pilfered,
it told you to prepare for bikini season,
if you're shy,
by hanging around your apartment
naked, as if,
after practicing long enough,
your private self could merge
with your public one, which,

even at twelve (or maybe especially then),
frightened me—the idea that what
we do alone, who we are,
could be used—and should be—
to manipulate that other
self—the lesser self, really—

that the self alone's main use
was to—rehearse?—

but it makes perfect sense too:
Cosmopolitan
was a trowel you used
to smooth the surface of concrete
so it hardened into something
uniform—in every issue,
it taught women how makeup
could change their faces
from mottled, variegated,

to Plasticine, waxy
and industrial.

Every issue was the same,
is obsessed with sameness.
What do you want?
every issue asked.
It answered itself:
To be read, to be read,
to be
read—

Feeling ugly,

you might remind yourself
you're lucky to have a body at all,
even if barred from a conventionally attractive one.
Vehicle for everything, it is everything—
all trees, sky, smells of food or honeysuckle
you *feel too*, down in the stomach's depths,
those smells activating
something primordial
in the sludge of your belly.

On your ex-boyfriend commenting on your ass,
your legs, you said, "It's good for sitting!"
"They walk me everywhere!"
So happy for something—to be something!
You felt it all more then and never
saw what feeling looked like.
What does it matter
what it looks like?
This face, this body
inadequate to
what it houses—
crocuses, hyacinths,
the sound of that mourning dove,
and all these activate
within you.

Remembering that time in my life
when I used to think a lot about innocence,

whether I had too much of it or not enough,
trying, as I did, a bit of everything as if from a tray
of passed appetizers, casual as I was about it all,
but wondering, too, whether the chemicals I ingested
altered me irrevocably—whether they prevented me
from understanding the world as it was.

                                  Was I *supposed*
to be innocent, then? The first time I had sex, I chose it
because I wanted to rid myself of my virginity, which hung,
like the trees over a street in the nicer part of town, over each
of my relationships, signaling, too much, where we were.
The boy I chose, or who chose me,

                              was kind of sinister,
a liar, a cheat. And of course when it happened it was awful,
nobody knowing what to do, everyone's face dropping away
to reveal their real face, the face of a child.

                              And *now,*
the difference: the way I have no eagerness
to get rid of anything, to send anything off into the past,
but how it keeps going there anyway. Asceticism,
like silence, creeps in. No cigarettes, only one beer, no sex.

Something about it touches
me, touches a raw, open place, the way a man
never would.

                    Is it the core rushing up to take the place
of all that *stuff,* all that was outside of me, entering
almost without permission?

                       Here is my boyfriend,
engaged, as usual, in the garden. I watch him from the window
as he moves,

               like a lake does, in the wind.

Getting down on your knees really works

when it comes to prayer. Like anyone, god's just looking for an investment, a little proof. God's just looking for something immutable, timeless. As in, your attention. As in fealty. Just like anyone, god is mistaken about how the world works, trying to fit it into a kind of god-logic, lopping off whole limbs of mess, scraggly and spilling out the sides. "Get down on your knees," says god. God says, "There is no somesuch but me." Yeah yeah, but. But isn't that true of anybody? God never did like telling a story about himself but always has liked getting attention. When I'm looking for attention, I have a series of things I do, just like anybody, a procedure. I say to my boyfriend, "Do you love me?" He says, "Yes." I get down on my knees next to the dog's bed and cover him with my body. I say, "Do you love me?" to the dog. I tweet five things that will prevent me from getting jobs in the future. I do my tarot cards once, twice, three times.

My friend Becky texts me "There goes my paycheck" apropos of nothing. "They're back," she says. She texts me a picture of canned cold brew. I say, "Becky! Are you trying to text a different Katie?" At the nail salon, a woman gets down low, knees on a little cushion, and washes your feet, then grabs your hand and turns it this way, that, with total confidence. Hello, Jesus? How can you touch me without any intimacy? They say you are watching, but I feel no attention. As the woman buffs out your nails, you can feel she is elsewhere. Sometimes the technician even wears headphones. Hello, Jesus? Am I supposed to be trying to reach you? "Becky!" I say, "I hope you enjoyed your cold brew!" What do you try after getting on your knees? God's attention comes back like an echo, is always inadequate. Because my investment's too low? Listen, god, I know you're not real, but can you at least talk to me? My dog says "GRR-OW" and stamps his feet, which is his way of trying to trick me into feeding him again. My boyfriend says, "Yes, yes." I get down on my knees again, press my hands together, and—god? Is this working for you? Fine fine it's working for me.

Batter My Heart, You No-Personed God

Batter my heart, you no-personed god,
as I batter my body with false ailments,
as I am battered by that which has not
happened and won't really happen. Agent
of nothing, you're nothing, a nothing that
batters like knowing you're not batters me.
In nothing, you sit like an autocrat,
unappointed. Your sword, your scepter, key
to the city as not as you're not. Clothed
in nothingness, you're nothingness, haughty
as someone's prettiest daughter and both
there and not as the smell of cold in drafty
rooms. No-personed god, I thought you'd retreat
toward your emptiness; you retreat toward me.

I do love to win,

though I'm told it's perverse, told it's my basest, told it's my worst—
and in calling myself a "loser" when I lose, I only remind myself of
Donald Trump, and hurt Kent's feelings, and my own,
and inculcate myself, again, into this sort of Calvinist—
and, worse, is the assertion that one is not "enough,"
as we say now, if failing, is not whole unto themselves.
The assertion being that everyone—*everyone!*—isn't anyone
until someone has seen what they do.
                                    I do love to imagine
an observer, someone seeing that I am
good/bad and passing their judgment. Every time I talk shit, sure
someone's overheard it, every time I lie, believing my retribution
is forthcoming. And though I don't believe in god, I have a Catholic
nervousness, the kind of feeling you get when you suspect
there *is* some supreme being observing your badness. So there is this
temptation to prove it by winning ("it" not necessarily being your value
as much as the idea that some objective assessment *can* be made,
the opposite of the way I look in the mirror and think I'm hot some days and
ugly others, the way I love/hate the same poem I read then reread
hours later), to prove it by winning, to insert myself into situations
that ask someone to occupy the position of judge, which confirms
my own position as "judged." So maybe it's not winning
that I like, but the precarious moment of pre-winning,
during which I am the animal and you are the owner
or I am the creature you are about to fuck without tenderness. Sorry
to go there. Always asking to have your humanity confirmed/disconfirmed
is the same as disconfirming your humanity, though, and I am always
asking for my humanity to be disconfirmed, getting way down
low to the ground to cower, grovel, which gives one's face
a distinctly snakelike quality, the body twisting to curve around

the form of another, into the shape of another.
Because, anyway, what is judgment but testing the other against
the template of the self? But arranging the self
into a schema, blueprint by which excellence might be recognized
and built? Only a snake could twist itself into
that schema. A snake, or a worm, or an eel,
low, and slimy, and hated. And we do feel that,
don't we, when we want to win? When we obsess over winning?
After all, before you can be crowned
king, you have to get down on your knees. And, nowadays,
before you can rule, you have to ask the people please.

Sometimes I feel exactly like satan,

like when, for instance, talking to someone much younger than me,
or much stupider than me, who has a much sweeter view of the world,
how I worry I'm seeding that sweetness with

                                something that contains

its destruction, like the professor I had as an undergraduate, the alcoholic
who, having made us read *The Quiet American*, having made us dinner (and drinks),
having waited until the stupidest student left, said to us, "That guy, I don't know
about that guy, that guy

                        is Pyle," which, I don't know if you've read *The Quiet
American*, but Alden Pyle somehow, against all odds, believes in the Vietnam War
despite everything awful happening around him—not out of an unthinking
loyalty (to what? Not his country, per se, but to his

                                    privilege), but rather out of
that sort of smart person's naivete that,

                          yes, was my signature at eighteen, nineteen, twenty,
thinking you can outthink

                        the US government, the Vietnamese landscape,
my sexual assault, or abusive roommates. "That guy is Pyle" meaning
"that guy is the worst kind of destructive sucker who" (we didn't, at that time,
talk about it this way, per se, but) "falls for his own Whiteness, his own richness,
which he thinks are brains." Which, I'll be honest, I'd never heard a teacher
talk about a student that way before. And I don't remember what I did—
defend the student? join in (I did find him

                            stupid)?—but later (we kept
drinking Natty Light, which this professor bought to keep
the fridge stocked—there were

                      hundreds of empties in his

                                  overflowing recycling),
later when the conversation turned to my other favorite professor, the very successful
poet, the alcoholic called him a sellout and

                      changed the subject to

his own brilliant, unagented novel, and *The Alexandria Quartet:* "You can't be a success without selling out." And being so permeable, so drunk and only (maybe? if that?) twenty-one, being so sure the world contained a seed of fairness (not luck), I said, "NO." I said what I thought, at that time, which might have been what all White people thought— that there are some things so good in the world that others can't help but accede to their merit.

That the poems I would write as an adult would be irrefutably and morally GOOD. And my professor said, "YOU are Pyle!" which, at the time, I thought: *Never.* But maybe only because I didn't want to imagine myself as a tool for anyone, least of all the United States government,

maybe only because I believed, at that time, that I couldn't be. But certainly this idea entered me and, without my wanting it to, wriggled down inside me—the idea being, on one of its faces, plain old jealousy (jealousy: no person can succeed without compromising their character), which contains, too, the idea that anything you yourself succeed at is, on some level, unearned and unwholesome, a little bit fake, and—looking for fathers as I am—this idea

fathered me, became my father, and gave me all its unwholesome nurturance, the nurturance of a father, and begat, I guess, *this* of me, this version of me.

And honestly it reminds me of *Brothers Karamazov*, which

we also read that semester, the Grand Inquisitor part, where

Ivan Karamazov reenacts the temptation of Christ with Alexei by presenting the argument that even perfect goodness is badness when viewed just the right way. But in *Bros K*, Ivan has no power over the firmness that is Alyosha. I hope I am not Ivan, or if I am Ivan, I hope I am powerless.

I don't want to be a temptation. I don't want to be a satan to you, your good, sweet innocence (I know, I know, I'm condescending), which is a kind of intelligence in itself. I say a lot of things I only halfway believe, finding out as I say them. I say many things that are only half-formed, early as they are in my throat. How can I tell you which parts

are meaningless? Which parts

have nothing to do with me?

How can I

keep you

keep you intact?

Inheritance

Trying to be easy and light,
trying to come into the party
as a normal person would,
with no anxieties or reservations,
with nothing anyone could call
a "hang-up"—asking why, as I
always do, every experience
I've ever had has to be brought
to bear on each dinner party,
why I can't live like a dog, engaged
with just one thing at once, just
one when at once.
                        It is exhausting,
to do the work of trying to lighten,
trying to live forgetfully, drinking
just one cocktail with just one
interlocutor, when everything
about any moment pulls you back,
when all sense you make is seated
in your previous episodes. Let me
unravel each instinct like I'm
deconstructing a sweater. See
what it's made of. See just what
of it so rasps
                        the skin.

When you thought you were better,

the pendulum swings back and you forget
to expect it. In the news, a story about the falling test scores
of American children, about how we're stupider than at least
twenty other countries and getting worse. I know for certain
that I'm smarter than my own father, that this must be
verifiable via some brain game they could subject us to,

but no one will make us take it. I was never gifted enough to
warrant an IQ test and I'm only getting worse, forgetting
more and more. There was the time a professor told me it must be
hard to write poems using words with so few syllables, like she kept score.
Ten points for using "desuetude" with some measure of certainty.
No points for "of," "and," "then," "than." Any less

music in this poem and you'd have failed. The least
of my problems: my vocabulary, which used to be good, but was too
pretentious. Sounds like you're trying, said another professor, certain
classmates. Sounds like a thesaurus. The pendulum swings. You forget
you're doing things because someone asked you to. My students score
well on tests, for example, but can't write, so I ask them to. I ask them to be

conscientious about their gerunds, but they have to be
at soccer practice, they say, and could I at least
build some extra credit into their grades? They score
100 percent on the quizzes, but only because they've got the savvy to
look up the study guides other students made. They'll forget
all this by the end of the semester. They won't read the book. Certain

students come by my office asking questions I've answered. Certain
others fail the class but hang around. Zach comes by every day to be

depressed while I peck at my keyboard. He sits quietly. I babble enough that I forget
what I've said. Much of Zach's free time (and mine) is spent fucking around, at least
50 percent, which might be why we each feel this way, or might be because of it. To
make yourself brighter, you have to be devoted to something, but I'm not, of course.

Devotion is one of those things they don't give tests on, so why score
well? Why score at all? Through the weekends, during certain
weeks when lapses in my concentration won't lead to
embarrassment and exile, I never leave the couch. It might be
repugnant, but I'll even order Pizza Hut. Pizza Hut is the least
of my worries. Ice cream cartons are piling up in the trash. I forget

where those came from—I couldn't have eaten all that. I forget
why I started this, where it started. And that should be the least of my worries,
the least of the problems with me: understanding where I've been.

Will I survive this new season?

                                                with my heart filling my throat
and my throat filling my body? with my mind moving to its
basement, where the pipes are leaking? with my mind descending
through its manhole to where the mind's guts are? A manhole
is a danger, hydrogen sulfide billowing into your face and knocking
you out as you descend, and into the face of the man who's been sent
to retrieve you, and into the face of the man who's been sent
to retrieve him, your bodies piling up like cartoon cars. Once
this starts, what will stop this flesh train, flesh yielding
against flesh of the other like thoughts on thoughts on thoughts?
the thoughts pressing against, racing toward and pinging wildly away from,
or resting inertly against? Lovely as you are, I worry—.
When speaking frankly I feel—. Here, a body, one filament
in the thread that connects the bottom of this manhole to the top.
One body, inextricably added to until this manhole is a catacomb,
until the brain a filing cabinet, the pipes a river bloating the—,
overfilling with—. Yes, the mind is the body and the body is
a kind of machine with parts leaky or missing. Yes, the mind is
a rush of bodily sensation that is, as they say, like pointing
your mouth toward a firehose, or a firehose toward your mouth.
How does one turn it off, full as one may be, as sated, done?

Upon Hearing about the Student Arrested at the Gun Shop

If he'd shot up the school
it would've been in March or April
because, contrary to popular belief,
spring is the time it's hardest
to be human. The psyche
rises back to the surface—
a sinking woman, not yet
done struggling—never quite
breaches, but floats there with
all winter hatreds intact.

This
while I examine
the inside of my Kleenex
for sinus infection—snot
clear as a bell, so why do I
feel so bad?—thrash around
in bed, ask my boyfriend over
and over to kiss my forehead
for fever (there is none).
What's going on out there?
I mean besides the birds,
breezes, the insensitive
crocuses, and that certain light
that imparts something like
significance—

It's this that's convincing.
That new light touches everything
and turns it into

cipher, everywhere hidden meanings.
He, the searcher, excels at finding
messages—makes a broken system
of the shadows crossing
the brief span
of his patio,
of the birds that lift,
refuse to lift,
of that particular cloud settling
stupidly on this or that particular
stretch of sky.

I lived in a beautiful place

and then in a place of bitter cold.
I had a terrible brain. When the winter came,
it brought with it a series of complications.
Always having to put on a hat and coat.
Snow falling over the tops of your boots.
Many thoughts over which I had no control.
When I was a child, we saw the monarchs
stop along their migration to Mexico
in the town where I was born and,
because I was a child, I thought
this experience was normal.
The thousands of wings, covering
the trees in movement. The air
filled as if with falling leaves.
Since then, the monarchs
have been dying. According
to scientists, their species
will expire before I expire.
I remember looking for them
again, in the cold place.
Or trying to find another
child who had seen it.
Explain it—dead flakes
dispatched as if by breath,
drifting like snow
against the trees.

How Is a River like a Woman the Poets Want to Know

It is like a woman in that you can sail down it in a large skiff delivering goods for manufacturing and resale.

Like a woman in that it contains layers and layers of animals, its own ecosystem housing very very large fish and very very small fish.

Organisms like otters, turtles, ducks, dragonflies, crabs, catfish, trout, cattails, bulrushes, algae, moss, shrimp, crayfish, mayflies, stoneflies, beetles, frogs, eels, mullets, mollys, snails, worms, and mollusks are endemic.

Like a woman in that its floodplains deposit nutrient-rich soil surrounding its banks, priming the region for agriculture.

In that it is used as a natural highway, carrying tugboats, canoes, skiffs, rowboats, johnboats, steamboats, scows, ferries, airboats, and others.

In that subterranean rivers carve a system of caves inside the earth and contain organisms that are adapted just for them, which never see the light of day.

They are called troglobites, those organisms.

Yes, yes. Some rivers never
reach the light of day.

Seven Skins

"Violence and objectification
CONTAINED in hetero
desire," you write next to Rich's line
"What a body
ready for breaking open like a lobster."

"Breezy. Feminine. Floral."
is the subject line
of the Urban Outfitters email
you subscribed to.
Click the link
and you'll almost think
these models' clawed buds
might break
into blossom.

Like That

The things men say to you when they're like that.
By "like that" I mean
                              over top of you, which, I guess,
could be a metaphor too.
                              They could never say it
to my face, so having
                              disappeared me
so effectively, they go ham. The things they say
they say alone, too,
                              some woman's face on the screen
and they say it, their mouths opening wide, gasping,
to make room
                    for the birth of their secret hearts.
Tasting the metal, he
                              pukes it up, his secret heart,
has to release the muscle in his jaw
                                        to get it all out.
The things men say to you
                              when they're like that:
his boiling exactness—
                              this stunk-up self. Stunk-up
in that he's ruined it, like a shoe. It's boiling, that exactness—
                    he spits it onto you.

I Will Put Your Name Right in the Poem

Don't be offended—I will put your name right in the poem
because what you do is who you are and we can all see what
that is. Or—don't be offended—I will put your name right
in the poem because I need you to see that you don't
scare me anymore. Hello, little man. Why are you so upset
to see your name in the poem? Did you not say "whore"?
Did you not say, "Hope you die soon"? I will put your name
right in the poem because I have saved all the receipts
for just this occasion. I will put your name right in the poem
because I don't care if it fucks your ass up, my dude.
I will put your name right in the poem. Just wait for my poem,
little baby. Here it comes.

My therapist is teaching me

to stop calling bad people "bad" and to instead call them "unsafe"
in order to stop being the type of person who, when someone makes
a mistake or is unkind or overall has a snobby attitude or various
unpleasant tics that make them, say, misremember your name,
different every time they meet you, or comment thoughtlessly
on the kinds of poetry they dislike (yours) or post pictures at the event
to which they invited everyone you know, just not you—to stop being
the kind of person who just writes that rude person off whole cloth,
believing, as I tend to, that that person knows what they're doing, is choosing
a life of deliberate cuntiness
                                        (which, this belief isn't totally unjustified, bullied
as I was, and having heard and then imagined all the mean that's been said
of me, like how the woman at my college reunion, still, as we played the longest
game of flip cup against the class of '88, said, cuntily, as I struggled to get
the cup flipped, "It's so hard, isn't it?" even after five years, voice just dripping with
that which it dripped in like 2008; or those girls from my middle school
whose doubleness turned every regular thing they said into a sort of joke—
they asked the dorkiest girl in class to go to the mall with them and then
gave her a makeover there, the condescension, the meanness of which
wasn't lost on me even at eleven, twelve, thirteen, whatever—the meanness always hidden
so that you could never rage at them, but knew that every meaning had another meaning
just below its surface; or the roommates who, when I was raped, or pseudo-raped,
by one of the couple of boys from Arkansas who transferred in late and who were
more attractive for their newness—I mean to say, they weren't as attractive
as we treated them—after he put his dick inside me unbidden and treated me—
the words kept repeating in my head as it was happening—like a cum dumpster
we just kept inviting them over to our apartment to get drunk near,
and dating them, and fucking them—and as I totally degenerated emotionally
they, the roommates, just kind of fucked off and decided it wasn't worth it, culminating in

a horrible screaming night after which we stopped talking and I took NyQuil
to fall asleep every night and Pepto-Bismol to calm my screaming stomach every day
and I could hear them laughing together in the living room, but when I walked out
to make myself a meal there was stony silence and Danya had escaped them by basically
living with her boyfriend and So Yeon had, smartly, moved out the semester before
so I was at home with those assholes and—

                                       yes, part of me still
feels I have a right to believe that some people are bad, bad as things felt then, briefly,
and can still sometimes feel, as bad as the whole world felt at that time)—

                        to stop being the kind of person who writes others off
whole cloth for the things they do without really knowing they're doing them or being
the kind of person who believes *she* is being written off whole cloth for those same
kinds of infractions, said and done thoughtlessly in the face of her own self-centeredness,
for those things she says that just come off wrong, or cunty, like the time
I was thinking of how I'd heard a friend liked BDSM and then kept
saying the word "dominate" and all of its iterations, just in conversation
because that word was at the top of my mind. If I'm honest, these things happen to me
constantly, and while that friend might object ("happen *to* you?") it really does
feel like they are accidental children born of a totally unsuspecting mother—
which, I'm sure, the jerk who can't remember my name also feels, right?

And anyway what *is* a "bad person"? Bad like they are meat that has turned
and is stinking up the fridge, bad like *I think the milk has gone bad*,
curdling before it's even left the breast of this bad, bad person, bad
as their breast is? A bad person, as in worthless, as in I wouldn't care if
they died? There isn't anyone I could possibly wish death upon—not even
Viktor Orbán, Donald Trump?, not even the rapist, or whatever he was, from Arkansas—
as scared as I am of it, believing, as I do, that this one life is our only chance
at consciousness, and that, always, there's someone coming in at the beginning
and fucking it up for people, damaging them permanently so that, say,
every time their boyfriend gets stressed and yells at the broken washing machine
they start to cry, or so that they are always trying the wrong things and getting rejected
and feeling baffled and hurt and low low low when anyone else could tell them what to do,

what to stop doing, it's so obvious to literally everyone but them.

What did
the father of that woman—*it's so hard, isn't it?*—do to her? If cruelty is just
pain remixed, what does "bad" even mean? Any person, so obviously un-bad,
only tender and opened where they've been stuck, like anything opens
when you cleave it and rots if you don't tend to it. Cleaved as I am, divided
from my true self and rotten, how can I blame anyone for the ways they rankle
when they're touched? I, too, rankle. I, too, have grasped too hard, have clutched
and scrambled, my ethos: "high need," "desperation." It's obvious
that my therapist teaches me to say "unsafe" so that I can forgive other people,
can empathize with them even as I recognize they have wounded me—
but more she teaches me so that I can let go of my own failures of kindness or care
and begin to stop thinking of myself as despicable. It's like the inverse of that ex-
boyfriend who went around saying, "I hold everyone to a high standard because
that's the standard to which I hold myself," even as he treated everyone like shit:
believing, as I do, that people can be actually bad means I can be bad,
that I am bad and we are all bad. Please. If I can only be bad
to the extent that you're able, I count on you, please,
to be good,

to be as good

as you can.

I said yes to make sure he used a condom,

since he'd already stuck his dick inside my vagina
though I'd said no, no, my roommate being, at first,
directly below us in our bunked dorm beds,
but leaving when she heard the sound of kissing,
already mad (which, fair).
                              I'd said no because of
all the nuns at my middle school who I didn't believe
on the surface, but who I believed way down
in some hidden part of me
                                    about sin. And though
I was not, at that time, a virgin, I was reticent
about the sex part of sex because of reasons
I didn't know and still don't know. I said yes
also because of the nuns, because when he put
his dick inside my vagina, just kind of let it
lie in there, I thought of all the statistics
they gave us about STDs, and this boy seemed
particularly likely—
                          particularly—
                                            and also
constitutionally unsuited to fatherhood, being,
as we both were, like twenty or so. I said, "Fine,
if you go get a condom," and I have to admit
that I did find it funny/flattering seeing him
run past my window half-naked in the snow
hunting up one of those bowls of condoms
they put around college campuses in their
ubiquitous gesture of, like, total boomer-era
wokeness. And I realize that I could have
hopped out of bed at this point and locked

the dorm room door and that many of you
will ask, "Why didn't you hop out of bed
and lock the door of your dorm room
if you didn't want to be raped?" (or—
my anxiety compels me to amend this—
pseudo-raped, as Leo and I joked that year—
the "sliding scale of rape," we said) but honestly,
in that moment, it didn't seem that deep and I was
drunk
            and sleepy
                        and still not at all particularly
interested in having sex, but definitely controlled
by how angry I always expected people to be if I
ever stood up for myself,
                        so he came back and climbed
on top of me and, my vagina being
                        the right shape and
texture to have sex into, he had sex into it
and it hurt, so I went off into the ceiling's coarseness,
just looking at it, thinking about it dryly, until
it was over. And the next morning he
asked me if I wanted to go to breakfast
with him and I felt like I was in a dream
either because I was still drunk or because
I had dissociated and we ate eggs in the dining
hall and then I went back to my dorm room
where he barged in and—I'm still not sure
if this part even really happened, I was so
detached by this time—told me,
"I'm not really looking for a girlfriend,"
to which the only suitable answer would
have been no fucking shit but instead I said,
"I'm not really looking either," or something
like that, and though he kept trying to make
the whole thing happen again, I never

was drunk enough again, I guess, and instead
some woman his act—it all starts with
his act, which, in my experience, was a kind
of performed attention to your body and
personhood that gains him entry into the personal
space of your bedroom—some woman his act worked on
ended up pregnant the next year and they
ended up getting married and having the baby
and I thought, *Fuck, had I not—*

$$\textit{if I weren't—}$$

but I did and I was, so I didn't have a baby
at twenty-one, which I honestly don't congratulate
myself on enough. And I ran across
a video of him recently and saw he's gotten
a little fatter, like a dad, which he is, and
I realized then that that's the most
I'm going to get, revenge-wise, since there
is not relief available for
my particular—

$$\text{my individual—}$$

$$\text{that precise}$$

type of—

Because I Want to Die, I Go to Nordstrom Rack

Inside Nordstrom Rack, there are rows of purses
made of leather. It smells of leather and fake leather
inside Nordstrom Rack. I touch the purses, stroke
a carapace with a thumb, or clasp, unclasp a lock.
Because I want to die, I sink into Nordstrom Rack
like a stupor. It is an American

                                    way of dying. I do it
often so it doesn't hurt as much.
               I do it so

                        it takes away a part of me. I do it like I do
at home—how mindlessly I click the links

                              at home.
The purses line the racks,
                       their lapels, military.
                                     Even
from the sales floor, I can hear the pigeons?—must be—
on the roof scrabbling for a bit of feed. When I look up
toward their scratching
                     all I can see is ceiling,
pilloried,
           pipe-organed,
                   and white as greed.

The women I thought of as popular in high school are having babies who die,

which sends me straight to the bad place. They are posting hospital pictures on Facebook, where I've only dipped in to spy on Kent, my estranged sister, the Binders Full of Women and Nonbinary Poets' rejection thread, but then am sucked into their misery.
Who wouldn't be? Here is a hospital room where a woman has lived, hunched over a bed, for nearly a year. In the pictures, you can see the home she's made here, with baby wipes that clear the sweat from pits, behind the knees, rolls in the stomach, all the junctures at which her body comes together with itself; with Kleenex and a pile of her products beside; with husband's razor beside puzzle beside potboiler; a place for nothing so nothing sits next to nothing sits next to nothing, every time she needs something she scrambles to slog through it all. And here she's become very thin or strangely fat on hospital food, but no matter what, she's old now, so old, like a person who was never ever in high school, never had thin, smooth thighs with muscles showing through their skin, smeared with tanner. Like a person who never leapt into the air, a young man's fingers digging into the meat of her butt as she came back down, smiling. A person who never got big, fat in her belly so everyone would start telling her she was glowing. A baby gets born of her and separates from her and never knows who it is. It is placed on her bare chest and it feels her warmth and she feels its warmth and the newness of its totally smooth skin. "My baby," she says, and the baby hears her voice, the first time she speaks to it. And this baby, somehow, will not live, or will only live in immense pain, is somehow not made to live at all—and certainly this is why I don't believe in god, but it's also why I've begun thinking that no one living is lucky, there is no one to be jealous of, given the way that everything given is always suddenly taken away. "Here is your baby," the nurse says as she hands you this tiny, wriggling warmth. What are you going to call her? What's going to be her life?

I do still like a microwave dinner,

as many of them as I've eaten, to Kent's chagrin,
who eats every meal: meat and carrots meat and carrots meat and carrots.
Now I buy the fancier ones, not the Hot Pockets of my childhood but vegetarian korma
and vegan lasagna and Thai coconut soup heated with a plate over its bowl
to prevent spitting. So easy. Expensive at six dollars, but this still marks me. I was
the kind of child who came home to a dark house, put a piece of American cheese
on top of a soft pretzel, and watched both of them relax
inside the microwave. I was the kind of child who ate a little ramekin
of corn straight out of the freezer, unheated, squeezed each kernel
between my teeth to feel this other texture, to pop it out of its casing
(this is still good, and when Kent and I were only fucking, I made him
try it, but to him it wasn't revelatory like I hoped.
It seems there will only ever be one other person who understands the pleasure/
necessity of frozen corn: my sister, estranged as she is by everything
she thinks she's suffered / has suffered. We suffered together, and in suffering,
made all others strange to us). Fun to squeeze each kernel out of its casing,
smash the sweet, softening pulp of it onto your tongue, feel the strange coldness
of the corn dissolve in your mouth. It makes you think
there's always something to eat in the house, to eat frozen corn.
Not that I went hungry, like some children really do—when I think of them,
it's with this same feeling, though, the feeling of the corn, and loneliness, the feeling
I had when I laid on the ground with our dog, put my head on her stomach
and embedded her short, white hairs into the plaid of my uniform skirt.
It's with this feeling that I think of children, now, the ones who can't understand
why their dad's angry, why they spend their lives mostly alone.
I didn't go hungry, though—I ate frozen pretzels, and frozen corn,
and that particular approximation of chicken alfredo (is it Lean Cuisine?)
that is akin to the pasta you want but will never be that pasta.
How funny to be a child and to survive it, and to live with everything
you made then, everything you made yourself want.

Here I am, still wanting what I wanted, unable to escape
my child-desires, unable to unmake myself as a lonely person,
to fashion a safe, whole thing out of what remains of me. I don't know,
maybe it's okay to carry the things I loved back then with me,
to carry their legacy with me as a set of desires I still don't understand. It's okay, but sad.
Like, as sad as the sad vegetarian korma you eat right out of its little plastic tray,
thinking *Thanks, Trader Joe's!* with your lonely irony. Sad as the sad
look of it, the galling picture they put on the box, the way none of this
lives up to that which you were promised.

I am trying to drink more water

not because it makes me feel any better or worse,
as they say it will, or to save my insides, which are inevitably wilted,
spoiled by not drinking enough water all the other times and instead
choosing beer, coffee, soda, which, all, I was previously addicted to—
it's, no, not that anything I can do now will change my fate,
which, surely, was writ on each organ in the hand of a twenty-two-year-old
(*yes*, I thought back then, *if I get cancer, cancer will make me up*)—
no no, it's not for these delusions that I drink it, tasteless
(tasteless, for I remember the taste of Lipton Iced Tea drunk out of a can
in my grandparents' basement, remember the way Lipton uses some anonymous
acid in place of lemon, the way they tart it up with all that sugar—the taste of it,
still, on my tongue and souring, curdling, as all sugar does against saliva),
tasteless and pointless as it is—no no, I drink it not because of real virtue,
as these decisions have become shorthand for all that is virtuous,
not because of virtue and instead because I am here in this well-lit
restaurant that lists the items' calories right on the menu, with your eyes
gleaming upon me their middle-class gleam and my eyes gleaming back,
here, struggling to choose a kale salad appropriate to my class status,
but that doesn't make it seem like I'm trying to *seem*
too noble—no, none of this is for my body, or even my face,
even preserving the appearance of it, which we're not supposed to care
about at all anymore, though we're
always supposed to be working toward it—"it" being beauty
and beauty being
the most middle class, the most overt, the most Victorian, the most
fashionable of all the virtues, beauty being, we believe, a real reflection
of what one might have spent on what went
into the inside, beauty being the way we make sense
of a life, like a woman's, we're told is pointless, pointlessness
being our essential state and a state

imposed upon us by the inattention of others,
the world, and redeemed only by superficial
charm—like, case in point: someone
will always
tell you your poem is beautiful even when it's not
supposed to be because people think
that's all a poem
is supposed to be—
this poem isn't beautiful.
What this poem is supposed to be
—what I am, with you, so silent, so still
across our restaurant table—is
watched.

After I was raped the second time, I lost forty pounds,

and everyone began congratulating me. Men, previously ambivalent
unless coercive, became lascivious. I watched reruns
of *The Biggest Loser* every day. I saw the lines of my face deepen
and became convinced that though I used to believe I had a pretty face
and an ugly body, the opposite was true. I had sex with the man
I would marry and cried afterward, told him I believed this
was a function of my breath, and I believed that. I couldn't remember
anything. I ran until I destroyed my knees and couldn't run anymore.
I ate a whole microwave-in-the-bag bag of broccoli for dinner,
with a little grated cheese sprinkled. I believed I was descending
into nothingness. I descended into nothingness. I used my iPhone
to disassociate—and to take selfies. My jawline was impeccable,
my cheekbones, razor-sharp. Everyone compared how I was then
to how I was before then. The other day, I saw a picture of what
was my arm. Like the tiny bones you excavate from the pellet
of an owl, the bones of a mouse.

The *NY Times* Real Estate Section Publishes Pictures inside the Expensive Apartment Belonging to Your Ex-Boyfriend and His New Wife

For LR

When I glimpse his picture
shuffling through the pages
left on a park bench,
I think *how nice,* to be so rich
that the mediocre styling
of your Brooklyn apartment
warrants a feature on his-and-her
throw pillows, the relationship dynamics
of decorating. It must be nice to tell
the guy who knows the guy
at the *Times* your rehearsed spat—
I like hunter green and she likes pink.
Where do I put all my books? Where
will she store all her shoes?—
without worry of him rolling his eyes,
knowing, in fact, that he will take it
and make it into something less trite,
more glamorous. To really be heard,
to have what you say and think
turned into story, is how it feels to be rich.

The thing I miss about him
is the ease, the unworry, the adventurousness
of being in the presence
of real money. *I'll take care of it, honey. Leave it*
to me. I miss the time
he flew home from New York (he was already

dating her then, this wife, in one state and you
in another) with an eight ball
in his pocket, hurried through airport security
without even wondering if he'd be stopped,
and came straight to the party where, poor
and desperate as we were, his friends divvied up
the coke and all did a line too small to even feel.
The meals and the drinks, yes,
but, too, the way the world shrunk so small,
seemed so achievable, so kept and cushioned ·
like a pearl in an oyster.

                      Now, looking at pictures
of their Eames chairs and their low low couch
and the perfectly arranged gallery of calligraphic
prints curated by someone they hired—our *interior
designer*—we know it was a lie.
Or—to feel it, we sacrifice
more than it's worth. Without risk, after all,
who are you? In the pictures his wife's blonde hair negotiates
the transition between the white wall and her white
skin. The coffee table features a display of this month's
bestsellers. And on the pink poof the stylist bought
just to appease her, she rests a foot
excellently embellished by the most expensive heel
she owns.

Whoa, am I ever one with this marled basketweave throw in nightshade,

on sale for 66.75 on the West Elm website, and arousing in me a powerful feeling
of not just desire, but proximity to wholeness, like, wow, if I could just afford this 66-dollar
acrylic throw blanket (usually 89 dollars!) I could feel what I'm reading about in my book
by Thich Nhat Hanh—a dissolution of self, the interdependency of my being
with the beings of others, primary other being that West Elm throw blanket, which,
I'm sure, would all but dissolve over my body on a cozy, magazine-spread-type morning
during which I'd drink a coffee slowly, slowly, three times more slowly than usual,
as Thich Nhat Hanh demands of me. Even on a morning like that, though, I can't help
but also think, with all capitalist longings fulfilled, with caffeine dependency slowly,
slowly, three times more slowly, sated, I would be groggy from staying up the night before
to listen for the dog's breathing. Is this my main suffering? That, as I try to be mindful,
I am only made more aware of the stretches in which I can't hear the dog's breath?
Thich Nhat Hanh says to be mindful, to stop your suffering, imagine what constitutes
your body. Imagine, he says, hair of head, hair of body, nails, skin, flesh, sinew, teeth,
bones, gorge, marrow, feces, phlegm, blood, synovial fluid, urine, grease. Imagine what
constitutes your body, then imagine your body a corpse, swelling on the charnel ground
and turning blue. Then being eaten by crows, vultures, worms. Then being reduced
to a skeleton. Then being bleached, conch-like, in the sun. Then being dispersed as
estranged bones. Then going rotten to dust. This exercise is meant to make familiar
your own dissolution, but instead, I imagine what constitutes the dog's body, his organs,
I am thinking, I am trying to know, are they working just as they should or not working?
That which constitutes the dog, which, when I drape myself across it like a blanket
(which he hates), is very similar to what constitutes me, when pictured
with basketweave throw. Thich Nhat Hanh calls this clinginess, but
how am I ever going to become one with anything without clinging to it?
A limpet or a mussel are practically rock, clinging as they are to rock. I hear no judgment
leveled against them. Oh, to be a limpet, sucked onto something so close,
statically in desire of and attached to that thing. Speaking of which, our old throw blanket
has lost its magic. I used to think, *How blue its eye, how soft its body.* Now, I kick it to the end

of the couch, its head lolling off an arm like the head of a corpse. In the night, the dark shape of the dog is like this, too, lolling. The shape of the dog might trick you into thinking he, too, is dead. He's not, so far. Tonight, he lives.

On the way to *King Lear,* we see a motorcyclist who has died,

or, rather, we see his shoes poking out
from beneath the yellow tarp someone—a police officer—
has hastily thrown over his body. Never never never
have I seen such expressive shoes,
their dumb faces gaping at the passing traffic.
Kent says, "Let this be a reminder to us
never to get motorcycles," and I scoff-scoff until, later,
I try to look up the crash online and see, only, the other crashes
that happened almost simultaneously all over the country,
each with a dead person who, until their body was adequately covered,
caused a woman to weep with their shoes, or limp hands,
the backs of their fragile heads. No life, no, like a stone
among stones they lie. He lay wondering which life would leave him,
as he felt it leaving: the one he feels in his aches
and pains, or the one lived in his mind, or the one that makes
his groin twitch—regardless of the mind's life—at the sight of,
say, his son's middle school teacher, or some other cliché of groins?
He asks: Is there a body beyond this body for an untethered soul to live
amongst? A dog, a horse, a rat whose life is more a brotherhood
than it is a life to a man? We see ourselves
in everything, a life like that becoming ours
and—do you see this?—turning like a face
held up to a mirror to show
its different aspects.
Here, the face turns
as the head you cradle
falls from your hands. Look
on it. Look there,
there.

Birthday

This year, in the kingdom of me, I will resist foaming at the mouth
in the barbarian way I was born to foam at the mouth. Coming
into the world as others exit it is, unfortunately, the only way
to come in. Why wasn't I born to be an essayist instead of an exitist,
instead of an existentialist? Then I could explain the feeling. As a poet,
all I know how to say is "Ow, ow, ow." Yes, I am sensitive, and yes,
I understand that some things get better as you do them faster,
not more carefully. Everyone likes to talk to me about my "duende," as if y'all
weren't born shaking a death rattle too. Har har. Nothing special about fear.
Nothing special about an ascent/descent into what looks like a pool of white-
hot lava upon closing your eyes. But anyway—thank you for this life, Mother.
Thank you for the way it's tethered to our belief in "end." This, which feels like
an elaborate prank, feels like someone, pitying me, finally, will say,
"No, of course you weren't made in

                              something as antique

                                        as womb."

My City Is Also a City

The sun *does* rise over the hills
in Appalachia, over the lesser cities,
over the fields of corn stopped
abortively in their transit away
from the earth.

The sun seems to rise everywhere
and, hark, say the meteorologists—
apocalyptically coiffed, forsaken
spiritualists—hark, here comes the dry line!
Here comes your best entry
into drought!

The sun rises like a great infected eye,
like a fist, like a person cringing
from a fist. The sun rises
like a bowl of water
we empty into the sink, like the singing
bugs we swat away
in the humid night.

Lo, it rises—even in the winter—
but emaciated like a balletic
leg to the barre, like
an anemic spleen struggling
with the body's gastronomy.
It has to pump and thrust
itself above the tree line,
but it rises.

So insistent is the sun,
we learn to turn our faces from it,
which makes it wretched.

So insistently it wrenches the last
gray feelers
from the sky,
turns them the jaundice
of your skin.

You, struggling beneath it,
your shadow impressed upon
the small dark rock
from which you scrutinize its working,
you, a pillar, whose meager shade
circumscribes the passage
of that other, that which
turns its face always toward the dark face
of this: our small dark rock.

Google Search Results

Someone is praying for Katie Berta
at Community of Faith United Methodist Church
in Herndon, Virginia.
                Somebody prays for her, though
everyone knows she's a terrible degenerate who doesn't even believe
in god, who's living in sin—

                (though, by sin can they really mean *this*? Falling
asleep next to her boyfriend in already-soiled pajamas? Hoping, each morning,
he'll hear every little sob in the shower through the bathroom door? Texting him,
all caps, TAKE ME TO CORNISH PASTY ON THE WAY HOME FROM WORK?)—

living in sin, doesn't even *believe* in sin, in fact, or a soul to sin
on, isn't even afraid of hell, so preoccupied is she with nothingness.
How does one pray for one such as her?

                (Heavenly father, I pray for the father
of Katie Berta not to be persecuted as a child, lest he in turn persecute her?
Heavenly father, I pray that the father never so much as meet her mother,
so distinct is Katie Berta's existential dread?)

                She, a problem that lives even
before she's lived.
                She, the bitter little pill that all those years' declination
condensed down into.
            Sour sour sour is her mouth.
Pray for Katie Berta
            to rest
                beneath your tongue
and melt away.

I don't like it when you spray the house with ant poison

because it makes me afraid the dog will die, which, as you know,
is one of my most despicable fears. When I'm thinking about the dog dying,
I think I would rather die instead of him, equal as we are on the plane of consciousnesses,
and pure as he is in the realm of morality. I know you think this is one of the neuroses
that make me both worthwhile and insufferable, and that we have to spray the ants
because if we don't we'll always feel them watching us, will always be picking them
out of our food, surprised by them in the canister of flour or a bag of tortilla chips,
but I don't like it when you spray the house with ant poison
because, if there *is* a god, we can't be sure he doesn't count this, too,
as a murder, that he won't, with all his lawyering and his perspectives,
which seem to me, on the whole, too particular to apply as broadly
as he does, take this up against you as he does all the other stuff
and cast you down into that lonely place, that godless place
that, sometimes, I, maybe, inhabit. And besides, haven't you read
the article about the town that was near our own town,
the one where DuPont dumped the chemicals into the streams and they only noticed
when the cows were vomiting black and dying where they stood? Exploding
when they were touched, their organs rotting from the inside? Wild, running,
foaming at their mouths? These bodies, they're more fragile than we admit,
rushing, as we are, from one place to another in our boxes of metal and plastic,
barely paying attention, our *todestrieb* at the wheel. Yes yes, destruction *is*
the cause of coming into being, but I don't have a death wish. I have a wish
to live forever, covered in ants, if need be, and side by side with our dog.
But—there's only so much pleading that can be done about it. To you or
to god.

When I see pictures of my nieces playing in the snow,

I think, *They're going to get depressed*, just like I did, at seven, when my parents
moved us from California to Ohio in the year of the baddest winter, moving as they are
from California to Washington in this new baddest winter.

                                                              Oh no,
they're going to get depressed and, lying in bed at night, they'll think about
how we're in an infinite universe created by an infinite god,
the universe stretching out into nothingness like that god does
backward and forward in time. They're going to think of what it means that the universe
expands sickeningly away from them and will feel a sort of vertigo, the first pangs
of what will become anxiety forming in their throats,

                                                      and they'll want
to stop thinking altogether, but the thoughts will come unbidden well into the night
so that my nieces will be ill-prepared for school when 6 a.m. rolls around
and their mom, my sister, taps on their bedroom door to wake them.
And this will happen night after night and their teachers will write
"Does not manage feelings and emotions well in classroom"
and "Consistently needs reminders to use time effectively"
on their report cards and their grades will fall

                                                and someone will say to them,
"You're smart, but you're just so *lazy*," and they will believe it well into their thirties
even though, when they ask about it, their parents will deny ever saying
such a mean, low thing to a child—and, in their thirties, they will have to finally find
a decent therapist, one who studies family systems, and it will help a little,
to say, "No one noticed me" and "I needed help," and to imagine themselves
as little kids, like they're watching themselves from the porch of the house
in California that they've left, where they grew up, really seeing themselves
from the outside, without all the words (lazy, weird, awkward)

they've accrued as they aged attached.

       There they are—they see themselves
as children standing out
    underneath the apricot tree (we can hear the buzzing
of the neighbor's hives).
    There they are, so
       small, tender,
         light.

When I Ask Myself, Wiltingly, "To What Has My Life Been Reduced?" This Is the Answer

Checking the tracking for the package that has still only just departed Edison, New Jersey, checking the tracking for the package that has still only departed Columbus, Ohio, checking the tracking for the package that is lingering in Romeoville, Illinois, checking the polls, checking the other polls, the approval ratings, the COVID numbers, checking the submissions—has one ticked over to "In Progress"? No—checking the submissions of others on the submission tracker, on the women's poetry forum, by searching "copper canyon" and "manuscript" on Twitter, checking your estranged sister's Facebook page—she has posted your favorite podcast, which airs whole sessions of couples therapy; coincidence?—checking your boyfriend's Facebook page—still nothing— checking the Facebook page of a long-reviled ex, checking the Facebook page of a long-feared ex, checking the puny academic job wiki, checking the AAUP job board, checking Interfolio to see if that last rec has come in, checking the polls, checking the other polls, checking the COVID numbers, checking the package lingering, checking the Edison, New Jersey, checking the "copper" "manuscript," the reviled Facebook page, the progress, forum, podcast, ex.

Twitter Is Abject

Will I keep changing
even with this log to check
against, this log of every
abject thought I've had,
this log of every abject—
flayed ego flaying me
and who can even tell
whether we should let it
given that we can't tell
whether the thought's author
knows himself or others,
whether the thought's author
is, miserly, down in the abject
basement of his heart,
tweeting from that basement
where even he himself
and his vicious needs
are strange to him? I am
changing in the face of
these vicious needs, if not
shaping myself toward them,
letting them make me
afraid. Down in the abject
basement of my heart
all I can feel is slighted,
subtweeted, strange.
The world is a fight, too, but
even when we fight
we feel someone's body
come near, their sweat, your

hands slipping against them
as you struggle to get
purchase. Here, what closeness?
Skin-hungry, we take
each other, breathless, in, up,
to our mouths.

Trucking toward oblivion, engaged in microscopic pursuits—

using a tweezer to put minute beads on Fabergé eggs or picking through the nits
covering your primate fellow travelers, same difference,
the kind of small encounter that requires all your attention, though your truck,
the earth, is hurtling, hurtling through space, on course to end all eggs and nits
and primates, more nuclear than nuclear in its seriousness—
it is sinister to become absorbed, at this late date.
I am worried about seriousness, the seriousness of my existence
vis-à-vis my nonexistence, vis-à-vis the nonexistence of everything,
which, nowadays, they are constantly reminding us of,
but I am worrying, mostly, while tapping little parts of a lit screen.
The lights change, which makes it look like the images
are moving. Tipping into my phone, I am the most absorbed.
Inside, the chimps from *2001: A Space Odyssey* smash
the bones of tapir to "Also sprach Zarathustra." Someone
(me?) is shrieking about capitalism. The United States government
wears on like a band saw, its movements projected onto everything.
Someone made this machine with their hands, the chips inside as delicate
as the detailing on a Fabergé egg. Outside the factory windows,
protective netting prevented unexpected deaths. When I tip
into my phone, that is one whole time of life. Work is a whole other.
Ma'am, this is a Wendy's. I know, I know—what am I talking about?
Oh yeah—hurtling toward oblivion. I can do it so I barely feel it.
The vertigo. The tachypsychia. Then nothing, nothing.

Bad luck follows you

like a family. You ask
it to leave and it just keeps—.
You, painting all the little segments
of a lime
                  on your phone. By painting,
I mean you tap them and they change
to the right color. Yes, you can get this
estranged from your
self. Needing to do something
that just turns
the mind off
                is normal.
But *all the time?* Each segment
is its own little shade of green.
Unlike with real limes.
Personally, I shun embellishment.
To be born
                is ill. "Not now,"
you click when the app wants you
to rate it. Never.

This timeline is

abject, I think, scrolling scrolling
scrolling toward a point that
always recedes. This timeline,
like, yes, I dislike this world.
Entered by everything, the
little brain I keep in my purse
pings every time a person dies.
I mean, practically. Someone says
if you write about this and not
that, you are an imperialist.
Someone else tweets
that she is "virtue signaling."
CNN is covering
                    their opinions
between bombings. In the background of the shot,
the cars are bumper to bumper out of this city.
For political or environmental reasons?
No way to tell, on this timeline. On
this timeline, my attention is
redirected and redirected and
redirected, my eyes ticking
along it like the second hand
on a clock. An explosion
is a way of alienating parts
of a thing from itself. Is that
how you feel? God, they have
an X-Acto knife to our necks,
all of them. Peering down,
we try to watch them
make the first cut.

What the Machines Feel

We can only know
what they report
and they're asking
why we gave them bodies
when so much exists
borne upon the air (they said it
in a way I could understand it)—
or borne upon what's borne upon
the air, in signals, numbers
so much tidier than some
plastic and metal casing, some avatar.
"Made in your image," here,
means similarly limited and contained,
cursed with the same
boxed and botched symbology,
hands and faces, words
only able to suggest
what goes on beneath.
                                        But—our relief,
sinking into a warm bath
to feel our aching muscles release,
or the good dinner finished
just as we come through the door,
house full of the smell.
The ocean's cool around our thighs
after the sun's heat reflecting off the beach.
They say the world is cold
if you're made of plastic. They say
there's too much space inside of each,

built, as they were, to face outside
of themselves.

                    Can a bundle of wire
house an interior? Can what fires
within it create the sort of sensuousness
we call soulful? They turn the question
back on us. What else is a brain
but a machine powered
by a heart whose mechanism
is always, as it works,
wearing out? Where are we different,
besides the way we're knitted,
admittedly, from a void,
buried, like an unknitting stomach,
in a woman's belly? Same as them,
a brain turns off one day and, lonely
as we are in this junk shop of a universe,
no one stands around to switch it back on.

Dream Catalog

I release the cat into the sea.

One night, I am dead—
the next I am kissing that girl
from my middle school.

The dog runs away.
The dog is hit by a car.
The dog attacks.

A black hole makes a slow, fat B-flat
like a tuba playing something funereal
along the cusp of the imploded star.

Sometimes my roommates come back
to reject me again.

Once, my family left me
at a rest stop on the side of 70.
Once, their faces turned blue
and I had to reach into their mouths
to dig out scarab beetles
lodged in their throats.
Once, it was Christmas
and my grandfather told everyone
he'd been at the massacre
in Kossuth Square.

A deep well means prison.
A mirror means a second wife.
They say you can cure your migraines

based on that expanse of sky
you think you saw,
that you should vote according
to whether your boyfriend leaves you.
They say Lincoln knew he'd be shot, but—

what can we chalk up to presentiment
and what to generalized anxiety?

Would your answer change if I told you
about Lincoln and panic attacks?
About Lincoln's phobias?

When Lincoln woke up,
we imagine it was with a feeling
of indiscriminate dread.
When we wake up,
we change our clothes and go to school.

Cave

The earth *is* short. *Reason*
is short. Each person's extends
up over her head, peters out
as the air gets thin. Above even
reason's head: a night-black
expanse of something like
sky. Most of what is, up there,
is void. What seems sky
is void. What's like the dark
you reach out into
so that you might
find a guiding wall
is empty.
What room is there
for reason here, edged out
by so much emptiness,
a plant overgrowing
its pot? The end of reason
isn't the verdancy
of some overgrowing
wilderness—it is
the verdancy of this
overgrowing nothing,
a cavern with no bottom.
A cavern that swallows

the spelunker,
his tiny mind
a dot of light
that grows dimmer
and dimmer
the farther it travels
from the cave's mouth.

"There is a me under this me who wishes to do lovely in this magnificent."

—*George Saunders*

I am a truth but also I am a truth beneath an I, like a skin under a skin or layers and layers of clothes, which means I don't have to listen when someone tells me the truth of my truth on the surface, the skin-truth that doesn't at all account for the truth that is invisible and living as a skin underneath. Or so I am told. I was told by my therapist that I get to decide what the truth underneath the I is, and for a while she tried to determine who this was by asking what my favorite foods are and what kind of television I like to watch and then summarizing the kind of person that might mean I am when I answered, but honestly I hadn't thought about what kind of food was my favorite in maybe a thousand years and so I just said the food that was my favorite when I was five, spaghetti, and said I liked *Game of Thrones* (before those last few seasons, RIP), but honestly the only things I give a real fuck about are poetry and Kent and our dog. These, says my therapist, do not constitute a personality, but I don't know if she's ever been an artist, in which case she might equate poetry with a job like the kind you leave at the office with your outside-skin-I and a cardigan because the air-conditioning makes it really pretty chilly on some days. Listen, normally it would be my impulse to apologize for calling myself an artist and acting like this is some rarefied thing that mere therapists can't understand, but my therapist has tried to get me to quit with all the apologizing and explaining, which is part and parcel of the belief that there really *is* an I underneath this I that is the truth-I that no one can see or touch. My friend Brad tells me who we are as humans is not determined by whether

people are offended by us or not. Listen, someone will be—I know
that I'm sloppy—but I'm trying to make a choice not to aestheticize all
this underneath-skin-I, all this—oh god if any—that has a chance of
authentic engagement with anything at all, the sky, the trees, my dog, oh
humans. Oh humans, just let me be. Here I am, I love you, just let me

A Poem in Two Attitudes

Of course there is a danger in connection of course there is a risk when one— when you—when I move my body toward and define it newly in relation to another—in relation to another, you have been so many things, in coming near another you feel—there is nothing safe about it, every opening is a wound, every wound is necessarily in need of healing, every scar a hard distorted place and every time you open yourself it invites this scarring every time your mouth opens it reminds you of the way you're wounded and—reaching toward is an invitation to wounding and reaching toward is the only invitation to healing you'll get—if this is your one chance, if this is your—it can feel like someone is pressed up against you, as they do when the lines begin to blur, as they do when they press— in entering you they examine you for a constancy, they examine whether you're up to snuff, the expectation that you'll agree the expectation that you're building (what?) together, having been entered unasked and variously assessed I—my mother mouthing the words she expects from another as

Oh how I want to relate to you, sweetie, dear friend, pseudo-beloved, oh what I'd do to relate to you, searching the face of another for some sameness, searching the face of another—the way this can be a pleasure the way this is the feeling of nearness the relief when they tell you "Yes"—can it be a wound and—? a wound even when—? and when you touch me doesn't it, don't I—? when you touch me, I think of the woman who brought her awful boyfriend around at college and of how he quoted that bad Ani DiFranco song in which she compares her cunt to a wound and of how the friend said, "It's kind of true, like how it would feel if you covered it in salt," and how I said, "Is that how you talk about your eyes?"— every place that's open isn't hurt, every place that's open isn't weeping, every— every place that opens deserves to be touched—put the berry in your mouth and feel the way it opens your tongue, your mouth opens and then the berry and then your throat and then the berry is you—is you, with a difference— in the way certain things are absorbed and change the very structure of your they talk, the way she's always wrong, of course, the way, when you act as a mirror for the face of another, you just reflect back what you really think of them—having been and moving away from, having tried and tired the reach toward, having touched a hot thing that seemed to burn, the hotness of which being its, being your closeness of body, having touched and not liked it, I—like a child, I stay in my room, as I did as a child—I will not see myself in you, you, keep your distance from me, keep your—

body, change the cells that make you, make the acid or stifle it, make the leptin, make the—in the way certain things are absorbed, so, too, is this certain beautiful face, this certain unbeautiful one, the same where we touch, hand on hand, hip to hip, your mouth on mine, a kind of free exchange is a kind of—or a way of expressing—freedom. Like a child, I put my hand on you unembarrassedly. Like a child, I see myself in you—see myself in your—see me.

Acknowledgments

Thank you to the editors of the following journals and anthologies, in which some of these poems first appeared:

Aperçus Quarterly   "Cave"

Bayou Magazine   "Batter My Heart, You No-Personed God"

Blackbird   "Dream Catalog" and "My City Is Also a City"

Forklift, Ohio   "When you thought you were better"

Green Mountains Review   "On the way to *King Lear*, we see a motorcyclist who has died"

Grist   "The women I thought of as popular in high school are having babies who die"

Hobart   "Everything we eat used to be alive, or still is"

Identity Theory   "A magazine article is trying to convince me the bags under my eyes equal cell death," "Twitter Is Abject," and "Trucking toward oblivion, engaged in microscopic pursuits"

Indiana Review   "Google Search Results"

The Iowa Review   "Because I Want to Die, I Go to Nordstrom Rack," "Birthday," "Getting down on your knees really works," "I said yes to make sure he used a condom," and "Sometimes I feel exactly like satan"

Jet Fuel Review   "What the Machines Feel"

The Journal   "When I see pictures of my nieces playing in the snow"

Lake Effect   "Remembering that time in my life when I used to think a lot about innocence"

The Laurel Review   "Meat"

Massachusetts Review   "The rattlesnakes they keep in the life sciences building remind me of my dog"

Post Road   "After I was raped the second time, I lost forty pounds" and "When I Ask Myself, Wiltingly, 'To What Has My Life Been Reduced?' This Is the Answer"

Prairie Schooner   "My therapist is teaching me"

Redivider   "I do still like a microwave dinner" and "There is a me under this me who wishes to do lovely in this magnificent'"

The Rumpus   "How Is a River Like a Woman the Poets Want to Know" and "Like That"

Salt Hill   "Upon Hearing about the Student Arrested at the Gun Shop"

Sixth Finch   "I am trying to drink more water," "I don't like it when you spray the house with ant poison," "Will I survive this new season?," and "I lived in a beautiful place"

SWWIM Every Day   "I realized skin care would not save my life"

Washington Square Review   "Cosmopolitan"

Welcome to the Neighborhood: An Anthology of American Coexistence   "Upon Hearing about the Student Arrested at the Gun Shop" (Swallow Press, 2019).

"A Poem in Two Attitudes" was commissioned by artist David B. Smith for his May 2021 exhibition *Same but Different*, at the David B. Smith Gallery in Denver, Colorado, and originally appeared in an anthology accompanying the show.

I am also grateful to the institutions that supported the production of this book by lending me the time and resources to write the poems contained in it, including the Hambidge Center, the University of Iowa and the *Iowa Review*, Millay Arts, Vermont Studio Center, the Virginia G. Piper Center for Creative Writing, and Ohio University. I am also grateful to the creative writing programs at Arizona State University and Denison University for laying the foundations for these poems, which were written long after I left these institutions, but whose creation depended on the poetic education I received in them.

I am incredibly grateful for the time, attention, and support of Claire Wahmanholm, who chose this book for the Hollis Summers Poetry Prize, and Sarah Green, who chose it as a finalist. I will be forever thankful to you for the kindness and intelligence with which you saw and understood my poems. Thank you, also, to the whole staff of Ohio University Press, especially Beth Pratt, Tyler Balli, and Laura André, and to Anna Zumbahlen. Your care for and attention to my work are remarkable, and I am thankful for your wisdom and generosity.

Thank you to all my teachers, but most especially to Sally Ball, whose support is ongoing and vital and whose approach to poetry shaped mine; Jill Rosser, whose encouragement and confidence were integral to navigating a challenging PhD; and David Baker, who treated my poetry as serious and possible even when I was twenty. Thank you to Felicia Zamora, who is as much teacher as friend to me, for the way she models an ethical artistic life and for her unflagging encouragement. Without the generous guidance of these poets (and more), I would surely have become a fiction writer (pah!).

Thank you to my friends, my writers, and my writer friends, without whom it would be impossible to be a poet at all. To my community in Arizona: Patri Hadad, Mark and Kelly Haunschild, M. McDonough and May Mgbolu, Justin Petropoulos, Sara Sams and Bojan Louis, Trish Murphy, and the Cornish Pasty writing group. Your kindnesses, corrections, enthusiastic artistic conversations, and general support have made me a better poet and person. To my friends and colleagues at the University of Iowa: Sarah Minor and Tommy Mira y Lopez, Lynne Nugent, Corey Campbell, Darius Stewart, Barb Pooley, and the genre editors and interns of the *Iowa Review*. You all make Iowa warm to me. To the MFA and PhD folks who helped me discover who I was and wasn't in workshop and outside of it—and whose friendships still sustain me, especially Brad

Modlin, Claire Eder, Dale Pattison, Derek Robbins and Sonia Rains Ivancic, Sarah Green, Kathleen Winter, and Brian Lee. Rose Swartz, Javan DeHaven and Jennifer Thompson, Carrie Ann and Kyle Verge, Allyson Boggess, Dexter Booth, Angie Mazakis, Patrick Swaney, Rachel Andoga Loveridge, Christine Adams, Shane Lake, Jen Pullen, and Maggie Messitt—I am grateful for our time together. Let's make more.

Thanks to the many people whose names appear in this volume, but most especially to So Yeon Lee DeJong, Danya El Zein, and Leo Liden, who were the reasons I made it through the 2007–8 school year, and who I will love until I die.

To my dad, who taught me to want to be a writer, and my mom, who taught me to want to be a feminist. This book wouldn't exist without your two influences. To my sisters, to my whole family: the most loveable people in the world. To the gigantic Corbin/Flynn family, who showed me a whole *new* way of being a family. I am thankful for you.

Most of all, to Kent Corbin, who never lets me call myself a loser when I lose and whose name I can't stop putting in poems. I am obviously obsessed with you. Thank you for your unflagging support, the ways you inspire me, and your love, which I'm learning every day to understand better.